Divorce, Hope, Abba songs, dancing and love

Vicky Johnson

BookLeaf Publishing

Presentation by *BookLeaf Publishing*

Web: www.bookleafpub.com

E-mail: info@bookleafpub.com

ISBN: 9789357440431

First edition 2023

Always my children Luis and Sofia. My everything.

My parents, Bettie and David. They are the best.

Penny- for always wanting cuddles, the best dog in world.

ACKNOWLEDGEMENT

Gayle. Who told me to get dancing
Mandy. For making sure I get to dance class
Tracy. For never giving up on me

Hope, comes fast and can leave as fast.
Cope, who do I rely on, when I so broken
Elope, I have dreamt of leaving, moving away
Slope, but I won't go down that route
Nope, I won't let it beat me
Mope, and I will rise stronger
Broke, oh yes
Awoke, from this mental hell
Spoke, my truth and live free

Forms, financial truth.
Truth from me, but lies from you.
Why do you want us to live in poverty?
Solicitors, legal aid, court dates and nerves.
The stomach ache and worries of lost hope.
The team of support, who tell me I'm good.
It's a formality to get the truth. A better future
for the children, safety and be happy. Let's hope
and keep fingers crossed for that shall we?

Year by year, older and wiser. Who knew I made such amazing children. My house mates, partners in fun, just sometimes I have to be stern mum. Not often as your so good. Growing up, finding your own path. I hope you remember your old mum, always here, loving you so dear.

I love my dance, it looks crazy at first glance, the music puts me in a trance, and I find I must dance.

My dream to live peacefully, be a fully qualified psychologist.
Live in the middle of nowhere.
See my children live their best lives.
To continue to help others, and stick up for what is right.
My parents to know I am alright.

Your not nice, I'm the best.
Years later I wonder why they put up with your lies and bad mess.
I’m free, your not. Your head will torture you with what you lost. That’s not me. I’m not for belonging. Time will never make up for the memories lost.

Little fierce one, I wonder where this comes from? Full of life and wonder. But there's abit of anger there. I know you won't put up with crap. And if you do your mother will slap.
Loving and kind, underneath it all my little super trouper and Abba queen, this one is for you. I love all you so.

My tall and muscular boy, full of kindness and joy. You know I adore you and love all you do.

My dad always had music playing, loud and good. The classics who lyrically had you in the moment. Dancing in the house , Elvis, Bob , John Denver, Abba, Elton and Queen.
One of my favourite childhood memories was watching Band aid and memories of 1980.
Music now helps my mood. I love music and all that is does.

Sometimes I still get down, I struggle with everything that needs to be done. Part of me longs to be a unit, and another doesn't. I suppose it's the fear and past trauma. Who's going to understand me? I've been through a tragedy. Abuse, mental and verbal. Things people say within there own struggles.
I will keep going, but I am not happy. I hope one day to be

I feel im in a battle with menopause. I literally have it take over my sleep, life and brain. I forget everything. Im slower than I used to be, getting older. And a hangover takes days to recover from. I take my vitamins, do all I should. Still feel it's unfair why us women suffer the way we do.

I feel my children have two lives, one of which im not included and do not know. I do not ask , I do not pry. I never wanted this for their life. They talk all to me all the time, but can have moments of silence. I wonder in their heads are they coping alright? They know they are loved. They can tell me everything. There's nothing ever to be ashamed off.

Strong women I know, who stand alone. No one to tell them what to do. And powerful. Each with a story to tell, trauma and pain. But loving life and smiling away.
Rachel, Sarah,Nicola, Jo, Tracy, Samantha, Melina, Ellena, Gayle, Gillian, Louisa, Natasha,Kate. Ailsa, Chrissy, Holly, Laura, Lorna, sharon, Sue, Tanya, Sandra, Marie and Mandy.
And especially my mum.
All those single ladies- parents. We got this.

I wish I could write something positive about
money, but nothing is coming.
I'm not superficial, live as much a I can within
my means but there always seems a need.
I work hard, pay my bills. Usually there's
nothing left for fun or extra please!

It's not personal it's business, that's how I have to see things now. I won't listen to the past bad words. That's gone.
The future is what I want. Smiles and love. With those I trust is a big must. I won't be with someone just for fun. My life isn't a opportunity to mess up. I will guard myself with everything I have and got.
If you want to be a part of that then you must understand.

Summer the heat in my face, and your arm on my leg.
The rose wine and smiles. I felt so good.
Shame you where not who you said you where.
That's it for me. I won't hang about.
Goodbye and get lost. I'm worth a lot more

One day perhaps. Lol let's not get over our heads.
Can't imagine a life now with someone else. I'm too selfish in me and myself.
But one day it's nice thought. Not a dream. We see.

My family and I. Which includes Hannah.
She's been a light we needed .
Thank you for loving my boy.
And being you.
Glad you're happy in our crazy home, Abba
songs, monopoly and laughter.
We are happy to have you.

www.ingramcontent.com/pod-product-compliance
Lightning Source LLC
Chambersburg PA
CBHW051721130826
49812CB00034B/1289
9789357440431